Releasing Your Life

Lana D. Tucker

Copyright © 2014 by Lana D. Tucker

All rights reserved.

Book design by Lana D. Tucker

No part of this book may be reproduced in any form or by any electronic or mechanical means including information storage and retrieval systems, without permission in writing from the author. The only exception is by a reviewer, who may quote short excerpts in a review.

Embracing Light, LLC books are available for order through Ingram Press Catalogues

Lana D. Tucker
visit my website at www.EmbracingLight.com

Printed in the United States of America
First Printing: August 2014
Published by Sojourn Publishing, LLC

ISBN: 978-1-62747-035-3
Ebook ISBN: 978-1-62747-036-0
LCN: Pending

Table of Contents

Dedication v
Acknowledgements vii
Introduction ix
Chapter One: Our Moment in Christ 1
Chapter Two: Hindrances 3
Chapter Three: What Do You
   Have to Say, Lord? 7
Chapter Four: Questions and a Word 11
Chapter Five: Obey 15
Chapter Six: Quick Fixes 19
Chapter Seven: You Get Out
   What You Put In 23
Chapter Eight: Actions 25
Chapter Nine: Lost? 29
Chapter Ten: Life 33
Chapter Eleven: Focus 37
Chapter Twelve: Perfection 41

Chapter Thirteen: God's Way 45
Chapter Fourteen: Righteousness 49
Chapter Fifteen: Things 51
Chapter Sixteen: Sow 53
Chapter Seventeen: Checkpoint 59
Chapter Eighteen: Movements 61
Chapter Nineteen: Stop the Paralysis 67
Chapter Twenty: Don't Forget Love 71
Chapter Twenty-One: Questions and
    Direction 75
Chapter Twenty-Two: Praise 79
Chapter Twenty-Three: Wrap It Up 83

Dedication

I dedicate this book to my beautiful sons, DeMaré and Tylan. I pray you have the desire to grow closer to God everyday of your lives. I pray you walk in love, operate in God's will, and show the light of Jesus Christ that lives in you everywhere God takes you forever.

Acknowledgements

There are so many people that God has placed in my life in the past and in this moment in time. These people have loved me, encouraged me, stood faithfully by me, never gave up on me, and inspired me to be the person God has created me to be. I thank God for giving me the best Grandmothers, Josephine and Mattie. They are true women of God who continue to live life as the light of Jesus Christ exudes from them in their presence.

I thank God for giving me the perfect parents for me, Homer and Gloria. My parents have instilled in me the greatest gift of all; they brought Jesus Christ in my life. They showed me the love of God through actions and love. I would also like to thank my favorite and only brother, Lee, for leading by example. For the longest, I did everything he did because I saw the results of his actions. He walked in the love of God and I strove to follow in his footsteps until I learned to be true to the person God called me to be!

I would like to thank all of the rest of my family and friends for your encouragement and support along the way. I am honored that God placed you all in my life at the right time at the right place. God bless you all!

Introduction

How much time do we spend trying to reinvent ourselves or our lives? It seems to come and go in spells, doesn't it? We receive a pep talk from a motivational speaker, a friend, or a pastor and feel that we can change ourselves and the world! Sometimes we read something inspirational, see a movie or a play, and feel convicted to make a change.

The truth is that many of us have that temporary "firecracker" motivation that fizzles out just as quickly as it begins. Then we have another inspiration and try to start changing everything all over again.

So what is the problem? Why do we keep doing this over and over again, without sticking to anything and changing things long term in our lives? Why do we tinker without usually even making the first step? Is it the fear of not succeeding? For after all, most of us share with our loved ones and friends our grand plans for change that start, well, tomorrow. Perhaps we don't have the energy to do what we think needs to be done to make a substantial change.

No matter what the hindrance is, most of us are used to instantaneous results that make us feel rewarded right away. Short-term actions don't always produce immediate results. We are too often discouraged that we have only moved one inch by the end of the week, or better yet, month, and we just quit. We should realize that those inches add up!

Yes, we do realize that the inches add up; we just aren't willing to put in the hard work and time to move on in spite of the small changes that occur ever so slowly. Yes, this is the same thing that we have already heard and we don't really want to hear it again, do we?

Well, it's time that we start making our own measurable goals to achieve in our own timing. We are racing against no one but ourselves. We have more control over the timing than you think. One of the best ways that we can move forward is through consistency. Whatever change we decide to make, we need to stick with it. We shouldn't overanalyze our progress.

Decide to not quit! If we don't quit, our lives can be changed. It is much easier to release our lives than you probably realize. However, don't kid yourself. Some discomfort will happen. There is work on our part that no one else can do. Start focusing on God's plan for you, be honest with yourself, and release your life!

Chapter One

Our Moment in Christ

There is no better way to start, than to whisper a prayer to God. Now is your moment, Lord. Now is always your moment. Imagine, Lord, if all of us, as part of the body of Christ, were in our "now" moment, what would the world be like? Our moments would continue forevermore. Every moment on the earth, every second, we would be in your moment and we couldn't imagine how much of your works could be done. Nothing could stop us. No, nothing could stop you, Lord. Of course, you know that. You know how important it is to be in the body of Christ. You and only you could fathom the works that we could do in your honor. Think of how many people have yet to hear your Word, Lord. We have to get the Gospel of Jesus Christ out to every man and woman in the world. It is our mission, and this mission is pressing. It is pressing like never before. You are coming soon! We are so excited about that. We are excited to be a part of your mission. We are excited to be who you want us to be because there are so many people to reach. There are so many people in so many places that we cannot fathom the number of people who we have not reached.

Chapter Two

Hindrances

So, Lord, what is hindering us? What is hindering the body of Christ from being where you want us to be? We are stuck on ourselves. We are stuck on ourselves like we never have been before. We know it is like that in the United States. How much so elsewhere? How much so everywhere else in the world? We are keeping your plan from being carried out. We are looking inward, for our own strength, but there is no inward without you there. We are not looking to you. We need to get our priorities straight. We do. You are the only one who can tell us what our priorities are, Lord. Why? Because you are the one who created us. You are the

Master. The Master with the plan is what you are, period. You have created all of us to be in your image. In your image we are created, and we are all different, so you have given us different priorities. Only you know each one of us and what drives us because of what you have placed inside each one of us. We need to stop looking to other people's lives and what your plans are for them. No two people will have the same game plan from you for their lives. Thank you, Lord, for even though we have human-role models, we remember that they are only humans. We thank you for the fact that they are operating in your will for their lives.

But then, how do we know if others are in your will for their lives? Only you know, Lord. It is okay to be thankful for the things that other people have done for the kingdom of God. We are to be thankful and we are to praise God for them. We are also to be respectful for the things that they have done. But when it comes down to it, what are we to do? Who do we have to answer to?

Lord, when we stand before you, we have to answer for everything, every choice we have made in our lives. We have to answer for every hurtful, idle, and meaningless word. So, right now, we make a commitment to you. We commit to look to you for guidance. We commit to look to you for every area of our lives. We look to talk to you more throughout the day. We want you to guide everything. Even down to what we choose to eat. Thank you, God, that this will not be a religious practice.

We will not be so particularly religious and rigid that we go overboard and feel that we can't move forward if you don't guide us to what kind of nail polish we wear or if we should even wear it. Let's get real, God. Let's get more real than we can ever imagine. Lord, we don't want a religious life. We want the lives that you have given us. You have given us everything that we need in life to be fruitful. You want us to be happy, whole, and well. You want us to live the life of your will, and we will be so ecstatic about it that we will want everyone we know and don't know to be in that same will and happiness for their lives. Imagine we don't have to just wait for life in heaven. You want us to be happy and fulfilled on earth today. This life on earth should be the hardest or worst part of our eternal life. But how wonderful you are, Lord! You sent Jesus Christ to die for us that we may have life and have it more abundantly. That is awesome, Lord. If we just look to you and obey, the sky is the limit.

We don't presume that this life will be so heavenly and perfect that it won't be met with heartache, hurts, challenges, and pain. We know that because Satan is in this world. He knows that this is the only chance he has to take as many people to hell with him as he can. The Bible says that Satan came to steal, kill, and destroy. So like James said in James 1:2 (NIV), *"Consider it pure joy, my brothers, whenever you face trials of many kinds…"* So is it fair to say that if we operate in God's will, that we will be constantly bombarded by Satan? I can't tell you the answer to that. No two lives are the same, and no two attacks from the Devil are the same, either. What I can say is to *"Trust in the Lord with all your heart and lean not on your own understanding"* Proverbs 3:5 (NIV). Acknowledge God in all you do.

Chapter Three

What Do You Have to Say, Lord?

So, Lord, what do you have to say? We thank you for all that you have to say. God has not given us the spirit of fear, but of love, power, and a sound mind. Anything that comes to us about ourselves in the form of words or thoughts that are negative is not of God. We should know that God is good and he is worthy to be praised. Satan is here to steal, to kill, and to destroy us in any way that he sees fit. Be ready; be ready for the attacks from Satan. I have heard so many times that Satan is patient. That is true. He creeps into your life and your existence with little attacks. Look at the things that are on TV. The media and Hollywood are slowly attacking the immediate prominent disgust that we naturally feel when promiscuity is forced on us. They make happy, caring, funny characters that relate to us in some sort of way, so we sympathize with the behavior and it becomes less offensive to our spirits. This is how Satan makes us less numb to sin.

We can hear the voice of the Holy Spirit. We are not confused. We can hear the voice of the Holy Spirit, and can be confident that he speaks to us. He can speak to us every day. He speaks to us lovingly in every way. He is the author and finisher of our faith.

So, Lord, what do you have to say? We love you with all of our hearts and souls. Holy Spirit, we open our hearts and our minds to your Word. We welcome you, Lord. Thank you for taking care of what we need even though we did not have knowledge of what we need! Thank you, tremendous Father and tremendous Lord.

What do we have to say to you, Lord? We are not shallow. We hear the Holy Spirit. We hear Him. We hear God. Let the words of our mouths and hearts be pleasing to you. God has not given us the spirit of fear, but of power, love, and sound mind. Thank you, Lord. Holy Spirit, you are welcome in this place. Thank you for this moment in time. Lord, we are confident in this process, your process. More than that, we are confident in your Word. Thank you, Holy Spirit, for loving us. Thank you for all that you do.

What do you have to say, Lord? We love you. We listen to you. We are with you, Lord. We are with you all of the way. You are everything to us in every way, shape, and manner. Also, we are everything to you, Lord! That is just something that is hard to fathom. We have a hard time fathoming what you have in store for us. You are awesome, Lord. You are the best thing that has ever happened to our lives. We are also the best thing that has happened to your life. Is that something that is rude to say? You created us for your pleasure, didn't you? You did not want puppets. We trust in the Lord with all of our hearts and lean not on our own understandings. In all of our ways, we acknowledge you, and you shall direct the ways of our lives.

Chapter Four

Questions and a Word

Questions, there are questions for God. We all have them. We all wonder about the answers to them, but what do we do to actually seek God or seek the Word for them?

So what is wrong with us, Lord? I mean, really? Why is it so hard to trust and believe? Why have we not practiced and lived our lives the way you would have us to? What is your plan for us? Better yet, what is your plan for me? We trust you, Lord. We trust you with all of our hearts and souls.

Lord, can we get a fresh word? We want a fresh word from you. We want any kind of word from you. Maybe we should stop trying to talk to you and, instead, listen to you?

Listen to the word that you have for us and for others.

How do we get a word from you, God? Yes, a word from the Lord. That sounds so magnificent, so wonderful, so stately, so "holier than thou," doesn't it? It's as if we want to believe that hearing from the Lord is so rare, so unexpected, that "A word from the Lord" makes us stop in our tracks.

As Christians, why do we want to be so uppity or so selfish? Why do we think that only the high and mighty Christians only hear from the Lord? We make it seem like we are in the days of the Old Testament, when the only way to the Father was through the high priest going into the tabernacle in certain times of the season or year. Why have we forgotten that now, as of the New Testament, the only way to the Father is through the Lord Jesus Christ? He is our advocate, our intercessor, forever going to the Father on our behalf. He is at the right hand of the Father! It's a new day! Haven't you heard? Where have you been? Don't you know that the Lord is no respecter of persons? Come on, and get with it! YOU, yes,

Releasing Your Life

YOU, have every right as a Christian to come to the Lord through Jesus Christ at any time, day or night. You don't have to wait. You don't have to wait for an evangelist or your favorite minister, who speaks to you at 6:30 a.m. every day while you are getting ready for work or taking the kids to school! What are you waiting for?

A word from the Lord! It is yours. It is yours for the taking or listening. Come on, get off your holy high horse and go meet God. He meets you where you are and will NEVER leave you or forsake you. You are free to have not only "A Word" from the Lord, but how about scores of words. The scores of words could turn into sentences, paragraphs, and then turn into Life. Yes, Life. God wants his sheep to not only hear, but more importantly, to KNOW his voice. God is not keeping secrets from you. He wants you to be abreast of everything He has in store for you. God is the most ultimate Father in the world. He wants to speak to you, He wants you to hear Him, and more importantly, He wants you to obey!

Chapter Five

Obey

Obey? Did I say obey? Yes, I said obey! Why do we look at obedience as something that we should reluctantly do, and that it most certainly means that we have to do something that is not fun? We think we have to do something other than what we want. It is like punishment, huh? No! You are thinking of the world's way. You are not thinking of God's way. God's way is opposite. Unlike Satan, who wants to steal and kill and destroy, God wants to give you eternal life, and to build you up in every way. In more ways than you can see are imaginable is what God wants for you. Dear friend, brother, and sister in Christ, God is your ultimate Savior. God is your Savior from anything evil and bad. God wants, more than anything, for us to have a personal relationship with Him. What? God wants a personal relationship with us? Does that sound creepy or weird? How can we have a relationship with a spiritual being we can't reach out to and touch, or even see? My friend, even though we have a physical body and soul (or mind), we are spiritual beings!

We are spiritual beings above anything else. The physical body cannot survive without the spirit being. So when I talk about forming a relationship with a spiritual being—the ultimate spiritual being and creator—it should be the most natural thing that you do. However, we have a problem. We have been catering to our physical body and mind. We constantly feed and nourish them, yet our spiritual self is starving. It is starving to be fed. What do we feed the spiritual part of our lives? We feed it with the ultimate meal, the Word of God. Yes, the Word of God is just that. The Word of God comes to us through the Bible. The Bible, although written by mere humans, was God-breathed and given to them by divine inspiration. Where did this divine inspiration come from? It came from having a relationship with God. That means they knew God! They knew Him, they heard Him, and they talked to Him. He was every bit a part of their lives as the life they spent keeping their physical and mental parts fed.

Chapter Six

Quick Fixes

There is no short cut. Think about it. How do you get to know your children, your spouse, your friends, and your family? How do you get to know them? You do that by spending time with them and talking to them. You did this to the extent that you wanted to get to know them. That's why some of us have acquaintances, not friends. These are people you may see at work or church or in the neighborhood. You may say, "Hello," or "How are you doing?" as you pass them in the hall. They aren't bad people. They are just people who you haven't taken the time to get to know.

This is what the majority of Christians are like when it comes to God. Oh, yes, every one of us is like that, has been like that, and may still be like that! We get up in the morning and say, "Good morning, God. I love you." We might not speak again to God until perhaps we eat. We say, "Bless this food for the nourishment of my body." Then we go about our meals and day, as if there is nothing else we can say to God. Someone may say, "Please pray for me." We will say, "Oh, yes, I will." We may really meaningfully think that we will, but instead of stopping right where we are, and earnestly talking to God, we keep going, make a mental note of it, and hope to remember to pray about it before bed. Because, after all, praying before bed is sacred! What kind of Christian would we be if we did not do that? The day keeps going. We get stuck in traffic on the way home from work, or rush to pick up the kids and take them to their football practice, or we may be late for an appointment with friends. We never stop throughout the day to look to God; we just keep going on our own power at our own pace. Then finally, as we tuck the kids in

Releasing Your Life

to bed, we say, "Say your prayers." This is our ritual. This is our sacred religious "holier than thou" ritual and reason why we are in right standing with God. We think we can judge everyone around us because we are so holy! If your kids were like mine, at prayer time right before bedtime, sometimes they said, "I don't know what to say" or "I can't think of anything to say," and I would say, "Just tell God that you love him." After all, look at everything He has done for us. (You know the food, the shelter, the toys, etc.) Because that is what's most important, isn't it?

Before we go to sleep, if we really are monumental Christians, we read that chapter in the Bible that we must read to get credit as a Christian, to be able to be an authority on everyone else's lives! Then we go to sleep, forgetting to say the so-called prayers we have forced our children to do, because we are so tired and have so much to do, and have to go through another day. By the way, did we remember to say the prayer for our friend? Probably not, and if we did remember, it went something like this, "Dear God, please heal such and such, amen." Now that was quite pitiful on so many layers, wasn't it? On a side note, come on, don't we know that healing is always God's will? Don't we know that he has done everything He can for us to be healed? We have to receive it.

I am saying all of this to say, "Hello!" It's no wonder we think that a word from God is so profound, something that we could never hear. If you don't know God, you don't know his voice when he speaks to you. You don't know to take a different route on the way home to avoid an accident or to stay at home a little longer because you will be avoiding something. How long are we going to kid ourselves, my friends? How long?

Chapter Seven

You Get Out What You Put In

Don't we know that we only get what we put into a relationship? If we never sit down at the dinner table and talk as a family, if we never hang out and make silly talk or ask what we like to do or not, how would we ever expect to get to know each other? Just as being an official family member is no guarantee to a relationship, being a Christian is no guarantee to a relationship from God. We put in the time to a relationship that we want to grow. When we are in love, we keep thinking about that other person. We want to know where they are, what they are doing, what their day is like, what their favorite things are, what they dislike, and on and on. We take the time to find out these things by being around them. If we can't be around them, we call them. We never stop striving to be a part of their lives and them being a part of ours.

How much so, then, as Christians are we to be with our Heavenly Father? If we want to know and hear from Him, we spend time with Him. How? Take the time to start off right. Don't just say, "Good Morning." Let me ask you a question. If you wake up every day of your entire life and say, "Good Morning" to your spouse, children, or friends and never say anything else to them until you say, "Good Morning" the next day, how close do you think you will be to them next year? Forget that, what about in 20 years? How much will you have gained in terms of getting to know them? For one thing, it was not a dialogue; it was a monologue. One-way speech is not a form of communication, so no knowledge is transferred. Nothing at all is gained.

So why do we have the nerve to do the same thing with our Heavenly Father day in and day out, year after year, and expect to get to know him? We know Him no more than the first day we say hello.

Chapter Eight

Actions

So what do we do? For one thing, we don't make it complicated. We don't overanalyze the situation. We simply treat God as we would someone who we want to get to know and love. That means sharing things about ourselves and hearing things about Him. The easiest way to do this in the beginning is to get in the Word of God. You get to know Him, His thoughts, and His ways. The Bible says His ways are not our ways and his thoughts are not our thoughts. So get to know what his ways and thoughts are. Ask God questions like you would of your family and friends. Say, "Hey, God! How's it going today? What do you have in mind for me to do for you?" Or how about, "Hey, God. You know, I have been a bit stressed lately. Can you send something funny my way? Can you give me something funny to say or do to brighten up someone else's day?" or "Lord, I have a lot to do. Can you show me ways to not get stressed today? Lord, can you give me wisdom today? Lord, I have a big decision to make today. How would you handle it?"

One of the best ways to get to know someone is to ask questions. Why is that? It is because they have to respond back to you. What does that create? It creates a dialogue. Why is that important? It is because we begin to develop our listening skills. We begin to listen to God, not dictate. We begin to open our ears to hear what he has to say about what route to take, to how to plan our day at work or at home. When we begin to dialogue with God, we are building a relationship. We are getting to know Him and who He is. When we aren't asking questions or thanking Him and praising Him, we are reading His words. The more we read His words, the more we get to know His ways and personality.

The stronger we become in those areas, the better. Why is this important? Remember,

Releasing Your Life

life as a Christian is not a walk in the park. It is not for those who are faint-hearted. It is not for those who don't have the courage and strength to say, "I can't do this alone." When the devil and his army come to you, they are out for the kill. They are out there to steal and kill and destroy you, your life, and those you care about. So when Satan and his army speak little things in your ear, like, "God doesn't care if you have to tell a white lie to get ahead," we can throw that thought back at Satan and reject every part of it because we know God. We know His words, His thoughts toward us and every other part of our lives. When this is the case, we have no confusion. God is not the author of confusion. When we are solid in his word, we are solid about what He wants for us. God is a good God. He knows everything we need and will give it to us. Ask and it shall be given to you. If it's not given to you, then you asked of the wrong heart, asked out of God's will, it is not for you to have, or the timing may not be right. But rest assured, God will never leave you or forsake you. He always has your best interests at heart.

Chapter Nine

Lost?

So what now? We are hearing God's voice, learning His word, and we are truly building a relationship with Him. Well, I must say, if you are doing this, then there is no, "Now what?" "Why?" you ask. It is because if we are having a dialogue with God, He is speaking to us. He gives us words of encouragement and love. He convicts us, not condemns us when we are out of His will. This means that He is gently pulling our strings to get us closer to Him to remain focused on Him as we would a small, curious child running away from his mother. The mother gently pulls him back to her to protect him. Yes, sometimes, there has to be more force than others.

The bottom line is that God wants to be near you. If you are talking to Him and get off the path, you won't get too far before you hear His words. His words calling you back to Him, back to where He is trying to lead you. He is leading you toward abundant life. However, as we all know, God gave us a will. He is not a puppeteer. He wants your unconditional love, devotions, and obedience. He will call to you and gently pull you close; however, you have to be within His reach. The more you ignore His beckoning, the farther you go, then the farther you are, you lose the ability to hear Him. When you are away from God, you can't hear him. He may be still calling to you and trying to reach you, but He will not chase you. You will not be forced to follow God as a prisoner. However, when you stop, turn around, look to Him, and move back to Him; He meets you, and he meets you where you are. However, it has to be something you desire. Once you do this, He has your permission once again to get you back on the path and lead, not force, you in the direction He desires for you to go.

When we look at a relationship with God as something obtainable, then to hear someone say, "I had a word from God," we know that it is nothing to be jealous of. It should be something that we understand because it is something we get from God each and every day of our lives.

Chapter Ten

Life

So great, we hear from God. He leads us on our journey to a place that only He can fathom, understand, and know. Is that all of life? Well, of course not. God has given each of us, as members of the body of Christ, an assignment. More importantly is it that we must do our assignments and meet together as a body as the day draws near when God will send His son back to get us. *Hebrews 10:24-25 (KJV) says, "And let us consider one another to provoke unto love and to good works: Not forsaking the assembling of ourselves together, as the manner of some is; but exhorting one another: and so much the more, as ye see the day approaching."* In the meantime, in our obedience to God, He will tell us what we must do. Maybe we are to be on a missionary team. Maybe we are to keep working where we are and give to a missionary team.

Most of us are not having a personal relationship with God, and because of this, we seek out His will for our lives in the wrong ways. This is where we lose it, generally. Why? How do we do this? Jealously. We see how magnificently someone is singing in the church or at an event and we become jealous. We become jealous enough that we try to think of ourselves in some position that may not be meant for us! It is alright to thank God for the talents of others, but we don't look to people to see where God is leading us. We look to God.

God has placed a natural desire and authenticity to carry out our mission as a member of the body of Christ. Just as the Bible talks about one body part not having the right to say it wishes it were a different body part or saying that it is the most important body part, so must we see ourselves. If we are the little toe, pinky, nose, or arm, then we are to embrace that as our assignment. Then we do that assignment with all of our hearts, but not alone. The body had blood, life-giving blood that flows to each of the members of the body. Jesus Christ is that life-giving blood. We look to him for strength, to carry out our mission, and to carry out the will of God for our lives.

Once each of us is doing our parts for the Body, then the body has free movement. It has free movement to go where God leads it to go. The body will then be able to touch other peoples' lives, to spread the Word of God, and to fulfill his end-time mission for us. When we gain new brothers and sisters in life, they can step into their role. They can find their role in the body. Just think of it as a lot of bodies going about doing God's will. We are going forth one by one. When all the members come together, the body can move as one. The body can't start walking without the legs and feet functioning. Therefore, the sooner we find our part, the sooner we can get the body moving.

Praise God. Isn't it wonderful how God has created such a complicated, intricate body? Yet, we don't have to know every part of the body and why God put it there. We just have to trust him, trust him as the maker, the creator, and the master to know what he is doing and to do our parts. Trust. Yes, trust is not an easy, automatic thing. Yet how do we practice it and walk in it? Daily! By talking to God, we are told the path to take. The more we do it, even though we may not understand it, then the more we see how God does not lead us astray. We then have more trust for when the next time he tells us to do this.

Chapter Eleven

Focus

Lord, you are doing what it takes. We should be doing what it takes to fulfill your Word, Lord God. We have talked about a dialogue, having a relationship with God, and being obedient, and sharing the Gospel with others. Lord, please help us to be the best person you would have us to be. That includes the spiritual first, and then the mind and body. What do we need to have to carry out your mission and vision in life? We really want an answer to this Lord.

One reason why we don't carry out the mission and vision that God has for us is because our focus is wrong. We can't have the right focus if we are too busy looking at everyone else. We need to stop judging others! Why are we so judgmental, Lord? Why does it seem that Christians are more judgmental than non-Christians? Why is it so hard to look to you instead of looking to others? Why is it so hard to do something for you when you have come inside of our hearts and made us a new creature in Christ? Is it that the closer we come to you, the easier these things are? Are we to seek perfection when we keep telling ourselves that perfection is something that cannot be obtained? Is it that we should not seek perfection, but seek you? *Proverbs 3:5-7 (NIV) says, "Trust in the Lord with all your heart and lean not on your own understanding; in all of your ways acknowledge him, and he will make your paths straight. Do not be wise in your own eyes; fear the Lord and shun evil.*

Why, Lord, is it so easy to look at someone else's life and point out all of the mistakes? Why, Lord, do we do this? Is it the negative, evil, cruel place from which we were born as part of the sin nature, which is huge? Why do we want to bring other people down with ourselves? Why wouldn't we want to shine and be happy when others shine, too? Why do we sometimes hate the person doing the sin instead of just hating the sin? Why can't we get our priorities straight? We have been looking down the wrong road. So where do we look? What do we do? Where do we go? First, let's thank the Lord for all that he does. Then we can ask him to please help us get out of this state of weary selfishness that is eating all of us up that keeps us out of God's will. It keeps us from moving forward. Does perhaps Satan have more of a foothold in our lives than we give him credit for? It quite likely can be so. We should rise above all of this and be the people God has created us to be. God has done a great job, and we need to give him more credit, most definitely.

Chapter Twelve

Perfection

Ah, to obtain the objective to be all that you want us to be God! To be the way you would desire us to be in all sufficiency! Praise be to God! If we take our minds off the old stogy desire to be perfect and place our trust in God to be like God, we ultimately become like God. It is not about perfection. It is about being a woman or man of God, a loving woman or man of God forevermore. Dear God, we thank you and praise you for your name, your works, and the wonders you have created.

Isaiah 55:8 (KJV) says, "For my thoughts are not your thoughts, neither are your ways my ways, saith the Lord." So stop thinking about how the world does things. Stop thinking about how the world does anything! Look to God for his ways. *Matthew 6:33 (KJV) says, "But seek ye first the kingdom of God, and his righteousness; and all these things shall be added unto you."* So when do you go to God? After you have tried everything and will "just have to pray about it"? Don't sound so mediocre and don't sound so pitiful. That kind of behavior and existence get you nowhere you should ever want to be.

The first thing you should do when you feel anger and jealously stirring, a headache coming, sickness coming, or anything not desirable coming on, is to look to God. Look to God! How? What have we been talking about? Keeping a close relationship with God means staying in constant communication, right? Well, we should train, and then ultimately, naturally, go to God. We don't go to God out of desperation. No! We go to God because we know him! We know he has got our backs! We know God! We know that he is a good God. We know that he is able to do exceedingly abundantly more than we can ever imagine! We go to God out of love. The love of God that surpasses understanding is what we can obtain. The love of God that guides us through our lives, each and every day, is our safety net. It is our ultimate comfort through everything in life, from the death of a child, to the betrayal of a friend whom we shouldn't have placed our whole trust in.

Chapter Thirteen

God's Way

So now we know to seek God first. What does it mean to seek the Kingdom of God? It means to seek God's way of doing things. What is God's way of doing things? It is usually pretty much opposite of everything that we have been taught, whether in or outside of a Christian home. It means go to God before taking the headache pill, go to God before flipping someone off in traffic, and go to God before lashing out to your children in anger. God will guide you. He may tell you to lie down for 15 minutes with your eyes closed while you take deep breaths instead of taking a pill or take a walk to cool your temper down. He may tell you before you try to kill yourself that he understands that you have had the tragic death of a young child. He understands what it is like to lose your own flesh and blood, your child. He may tell you to go to grief counseling. He may tell you to call up that friend who you have lost touch with, the friend who used to listen to you and not judge you, but just love you and support you in your crisis. Sometimes, God will lead you to go to the doctor, sometimes not.

The point is this: No matter what the action that is to be taken, or you think it is, go to God first. If you have a regular conversation with Him every day, this won't be so difficult. It is a lot easier to practice using the brakes of the car before that animal runs out in front of you on the road, isn't it? Ask God for ways to grow closer. Ask God how to maximize your time.

Ask God how to be an example through your actions, not by slamming the Word down someone's throat who doesn't know you. Ask God for you to be that example, that person who people come to for advice or direction, or just to have someone listen to them even if they don't know why they are coming to you. One day, they may just ask you, "Why is it you are the way you are?" As Joyce Meyer, one of my favorite evangelists, said, don't just go around with your Jesus jewelry and your bumper stickers that brag about how big of a Christian you are, trying to be seen by strangers around you that you are a Christian. Your actions are your testimony to others. Joyce said something like this, "Witness to those around you, and sometimes use words!" I absolutely love that!

You can talk all day about who you are in Christ, but the world has to see to believe. If they see you acting the same, cussing, being quick to anger, cheating on your time at work, and gossiping about others, what in the world do you think you have to offer them? You have nothing! Instead of saying that you are a Christian, you would be better off keeping your mouth shut! Now am I saying "act" perfect, or "act" like you are "holier than thou"? Absolutely not! Here we go again, thinking like the world, which is not God's way of doing things. We are instead to keep a real relationship with Christ and let him lead our lives.

As he leads our lives and we become more like him, we become something real. That something is a true believer in Christ, a true follower of the Holy Spirit, and a true Child of God! Thank you, Lord!

Chapter Fourteen

Righteousness

How does the righteousness come in? We can't do enough to become righteous. Thank God, his mercy endures. His mercy endures forever. At church, we say this at the end of every service: "For the Lord is Good, and His Mercy Endures Forever." Praise God for that. We don't earn righteousness. Jesus died on the cross for us so that we may be seen as righteous through all of the works that HE did, not we did. That is the best news! By seeking God's way of doing things, you are indeed seeking his righteousness automatically. Isn't that awesome? I love those automatic blessings! Don't you? It is great and it is fabulous!

So what do we have from here? We are going to God then we look at his way of doing things, which, in essence, is seeking his automatic righteousness. Then what happens? All of these things shall be added to you!

Chapter Fifteen

Things

What in the world are all of these things? What are all of these things? In Matthew, it talks about not worrying because God knows our needs. We are not to worry about what we shall eat or what we shall wear. *Matthew 6:25 (KJV) specifically says, "Therefore I say unto you, Take no thought for your life, what ye shall eat, or what ye shall drink; nor yet for your body, what ye shall put on. Is not the life more than meat, and the body than raiment?"* We could look at things as provisions. God knows that we need shelter, to eat, and wear clothes. God knows that we need them, so he promises to provide them. God knows that we need the basic things in life in order to live. He will provide each of us with what He considers to be necessary.

Well, what else is there? The sky is the limit! God wants to give good things to his children. He does not want to see you lacking or to be without. When you are putting God and his way of doing things first in your life, look out! He is able to exceedingly, abundantly do all that we could ever imagine. This is just for doing things his way. We haven't even asked him for anything yet, most likely. Even so, when you ask for things that are not out of the will of God, God will give you your desires, the desires of your heart! It can be anything from giving birth to a child, the longing to adopt a special-needs child, a fancy purse, money to give to more charities, money to meet the needs of another household, to buy a muscle car, or even a castle. Yes, it may seem out of reach, but there are so many ways that God is looking to take care of His children. We are children of the King and we live royally.

Chapter Sixteen

Sow

Now I don't want to make it sound like God is a willing "genie." Absolutely not! God's way of doing things means that we have to do what he tells us to do. One of the biggest things we need to do on our behalf is to sow into His Kingdom, sow into the Kingdom of God. Yes, I said it! Yes, I went there! Yes, I mean financially!

God has laws and principles that we must follow. The best thing you could learn to make your life as God would have it is to recognize the law of seedtime and harvest. This is an incredible law that works. It works for every Christian. God is not mocked; what you sow, you reap. In other words, don't expect to plant seeds for corn and get an apple tree. We can sow our time to people in need. We can sow our gift of words in writing. We can sow our talent of playing an instrument at church. We can sow our physical strength in cutting grass for the single parent or elderly neighbor. We have endless ways of sowing in our life. But, the biggest thing people fear but know is that when it comes to money, what you sow is what you reap. You sow sparingly then you reap sparingly. God has placed this system for us because it is his way of doing things. This is how God takes care of our basic needs.

So in order to be financially independent and to be in God's will, you must always tithe! Yes, I mean 10 percent of your gross not net income. If you sow sparingly, you reap sparingly. God even dares you. He says do this and see if He doesn't open a window of blessings in your life. Tithing is the least you can do to be in God's will for your life when it comes to his provision, God's provision for your life.

If you really want to get fancy with your giving, what do you do? You give an offering too! What? Yes, I said it and I said it out loud! Offerings give God the open door to not just take care of your basic needs, but abundance for your life. Please don't be selfish and say that all you need to do or want to do is tithe for your basic needs! Come on now! Think like God thinks! Think God's way, God's system of doing things! God has all that we could ever dare to need or want for our lives. God's way of doing things is taking care of others. In order to take care of others, you need to have more than your basic needs, right? Go ahead, just live on your basic needs if that's your heart's desire, but don't be so stingy that you can't ask God to give you more so you can bless others. I think it would be awesome if God blessed me so much that I was able to live on 10 percent and give 90 percent! Now that's what I call leading a life in Christ.

Why shouldn't we, as Christians, have so much financial overflow that when a family having hard times with no place to live safely needs a place to live, we say, "Here, take this. I have paid the first year's rent for your apartment or home"? Go forth, give to others as God gave to you and be prosperous. What about the child from Cambodia who needs a life-saving surgery? Don't you dare get unrighteous and say, "Well, the family should just pray for healing!" How dare you! Whether the family knows Christ or not, every one of us is given a different measure of faith. We are not to judge our brothers or sisters because they don't have the faith that we claim to have, and really probably don't have. My problems and thorns in my side are not the same as yours. Don't you dare judge where someone else is in Christ!

The love of God shown by paying for that child's life-saving surgery plants a seed! Remember that seeds are not only financial. This was a seed of the love of Jesus Christ sown into this family's life. This opens their hearts. Opens their hearts to what? It opens their hearts to hear to the Gospel of Jesus Christ. What a way of being in love and showing God's love. Even if this family does not accept Christ, I guarantee that when the next act or love or Christ is shown to them, their hearts will open just a little bit more. A little bit more because now, someone has watered your seed. Yes, just as physical seeds need watering, so do the seeds we sow for Christ. The seeds are watered, then grow, and eventually become what God had created them to be. So do you see how your act of offering can help? Can you see how thinking beyond yourself to others is what the love of Christ is all about?

Chapter Seventeen

Checkpoint

Look at this! We have learned that a word from God is not magic. It is not something that is impossible to obtain. We know because God is not a respecter of persons that all of us can build a personal relationship with God, who is a spiritual God, because we are created in his image and are spiritual beings as well.

Once we have and continue to grow in that relationship, we start looking to God first in all that we do, from when to go to the grocery store, whether to home school our children or send them to public or private school, to what time to leave for our vacation! We learned that by seeking God, we are seeking his way of doing so in righteousness, and all things will be given to us.

We know that God is not magic. God is real and he gives us responsibilities. He has given us the responsibility of using his law of sowing and reaping in our lives. When you sow the time you spend reading to your grandmother, you are sowing the love of God and expectation that someone you love will do the same for you when you are older. When you help someone besides yourself get a job, you are sowing for yourself as well. You are sowing and expecting that when or if you are faced with losing a job or leaving one due to not agreeing to the ethics of the company, God will provide for you as well.

God is our provider. He wants us to be happy, succeed, and live a life of abundance.

Chapter Eighteen

Movements

Are you stuck? Do you wonder what you are going to do with all of this information? How are you going to start? Well, let's see, you are going to go to God first! He will lead and guide you to what he has in store for your life. He knows what's ahead, not you.

This is where trusting him comes in. I trust in the Lord with all of my heart and lean not unto my own understanding! Don't give up, but give it to God! Don't let yourself fall by the wayside because your neighbor spends five hours in the morning in the Word and prayer. I tell you, some people are called to do that and God gives them the

Grace to do that. However, if you do that, and God has not shared with you to do it, you are out of his will; you will be extremely frustrated, and quit, feeling condemned. You can't mimic God's will for someone else's life. Please don't go there! I know that it's so easy to do.

I have been torn by what I see others do my whole life. It never benefited me. It made me feel sorry for myself and get nowhere but holed up in a corner, thinking bad thoughts about myself and my worthlessness. Please don't do this.

God may start you small. This is how he started me. I received a daily devotional called the *Upper Room*. It was a gift from my father. I did not expect it and didn't really think much of it. You know how it is. When you are a Christian, people you love respect that and look for ways to bless you and help you grow. At that time, I was not even thinking about reading my Bible daily. Well, I take that back. I was thinking of reading my Bible daily; I just wasn't doing it.

At the beginning of the year, God impressed upon me to open the *Upper Room* booklet and read it. I thought, *Well, I am a Holy Spirit-filled Christian. How is some little book for baby Christian's going to change my life?* Boy did God have a big laugh on that attitude!

Each day was the perfect portion of what I needed to get my day started and reading the Word of God. I went from reading the Bible verses quoted on Sunday while in church to reading the Bible daily through the devotions in my booklet. Now my day started with some verses to read in the Bible, followed by scripture references. I was able to bite off the Word of God in small pieces. These pieces led me to be able to really think about and meditate on the Word.

Next, there would be people sharing their own testimonies. Sharing their testimonies of how perhaps God placed someone, sometimes a child, in their lives in a particular way to view the Word of God and God in some way that they had not yet seen or thought about before. Not only this, but these people were from all over the world. I got to the point where I would try to guess where they were from each day as I read.

God showed me how Christians all over the world have the same experiences and challenges in their lives. Not only that, but I was reading the same scriptures and having the same prayers as Christians all over the world, on the same day! We were all united as one. Now <u>that</u> is unity as the body of Christ!

God showed me that all of us all over the world are indeed made in Christ's image. For how could so many different people with so many different backgrounds come to know God and become examples of the love of God to others? No matter what faith they were, no matter if they traveled far to go to church, or had meetings in their homes, the love of Christ was shown the same.

I was so humbled. I continue to be humbled. God used my father to give me a little booklet, a little booklet that is leading me to study God's Word, and it gives me testimony after testimony of how God's Love is universal. Just think how much of the Word of God I have read from that little devotional on a regular basis to only the Word I read *if* I were in church on Sunday! God is good!

Releasing Your Life

God is so good. Never underestimate how people can do the smallest things to change your lives! God is not surrounded by a box or by the world's way of doing things. He meets you where you are! He meets you where you are not reading his Word, and the next thing you know, he has you reading his Word. He is not judging you for reading only a tiny portion of it every day; he is celebrating you for taking the time to get to know him, to get to know him on a most personal level. Ten minutes of reading and meditating on God's word daily to draw near to him versus reading the Bible with a checklist so you can say that you read the entire Bible in one year, without giving God a second thought, are not to be compared.

GOD IS NOT MOCKED! WHATSOEVER YOU SOW, YOU SHALL REAP! Do you want to sow yourself and your time to God to get to know him more and more each and every day, or do you want to sow reading the most chapters you can so you can quote scripture, yet don't know and don't have it applied to your life? Think about it! BE REAL! GOD IS NOT MOCKED! WHATSOEVER YOU SOW,

YOU SHALL REAP! I am in no way putting down Bible-reading programs and lists that help us stay disciplined!

What I am saying is to do things with your heart. God knows your motive; you cannot deceive him. There is no need to try to fool him or yourself. Sometimes, you may need to slow down to get yourself right back up to speed, right? As long as you ask God what to do and how to do it, and to do it with the heart and love of God, you will be blessed. It is my deepest desire to go before the Father and hear him say, "Well done, my faithful servant." That is my desire for you.

Thank you, Father, for what you have shown us today. Thank you for all you do. You are our source of provision and love. We praise your name and thank you!

Chapter Nineteen

Stop the Paralysis

Let's get back to what continues to hold us up in our lives. We keep getting off the path, over and over again. We are frightened and keep holding over our own heads that we are not, but need to be in God's will. We keep saying it so much that we are paralyzed in our tracks or keep trying all of the roads ahead, only to have to come back to where we started and try all over again. We are paralyzed because we keep thinking that we don't hear from God. Why are we so hung up on these things, Lord? What is it that we need to do? Is being in your will such a hard thing to grasp?

Perhaps we should break it down to something easier, yet truthful. What does being in God's will mean to you and me? Just remember, it means that we talk to and communicate with God all of the time. It is like praying without ceasing. It means that because we communicate with God all of the time, we have asked where he wants us, from what time to go to work, to what job to be in, to how much time do we spend off from work to be with our children, to sensing the needs of our children, to when to take a friend to lunch.

Am I saying that to be in God's will is like slavery? No way! Just because I string a list of examples together about things we can be talking to God about, let's not get super-righteous. I am not saying that you stand in your closet until God tells you what to wear. Being in God's will doesn't mean that I do not have a will. God gave us our will! He wants us to have it! This is the difference between serving God because we love and desire him and serving God only to do so because we are afraid or feel forced to. When we mention our wills, we usually do so in a negative way. We think it means that we are being rebellious or defiant, or we have an ugly, naughty nature.

Let's remember this, though: If God gave it to us, it is good and he has intended it for good, rather than we understand why he did it or not. When you become more like Christ and exercise your own FREE (not forced) will, it can be a beautiful thing. Why is that? The closer you are to Christ, the closer you are to Him and His desires. This means that when you are in God's will, you can still be in your will, too. It is kind of like not making the mistake of asking amiss. If you exercise your will to sell illegal drugs because you can make a lot of money and take care of your church, don't kid yourself. God would not bless or have you to do something illegal.

Give God credit. He has a million legal ways to get you what you need. Your will should be in line with God's Word, which is God's will, not the other way around. We don't exercise our will and expect God to give in to us! No! It doesn't work like that. God is a God of order and organization! In order to have organization, something must be at the top! What or who is at the top? You? Absolutely not!

God is at the top and please don't forget it. He is right there where you can find him all of the time. You always know where to find him. He will never leave you or forsake you. The joy of the Lord is our strength!

Chapter Twenty

Don't Forget Love

We have highlighted God's Will, having a relationship with God, seeking first the kingdom of God and all of these things will be added to you. There are so many basic things that we have covered. Another basic is walking in love. Oh, did I go there? Yes, I did.

Being in a relationship with God is impossible if you have no love, because God is Love. To be in love is to keep growing in God, keep growing in your relationship with him. To know God is to read His Word. When you read His Word, you can see the ways that God walked in Love. When you see how Christ was by the examples of his actions in the Bible, you can see what it means to live on earth and walk in Love.

Only a God as good as our God would humble himself and come in the form of a man to walk with man, to die for man, and to save us from our sins. He was the epitome of a sinless life. He lived a life on this earth, walking in love, without sin, and dealing with the sinful ways of men and life. There is nothing he didn't go through that we can't learn from.

Think of Jesus being tempted by Satan. Everything Satan said to Jesus was answered by Jesus with the Word of God. That was like seeping hot coal upon his head. When in doubt, go to the Word of God. If you don't know the Word of God from reading the Word of God, how can you attack Satan and his cronies? You can't, and then you are more likely to be in fear.

Fear is not from God. God has not given us the spirit of Fear but of power, and of love and of a sound mind. So walking in love is something we can learn by following the examples of Jesus Christ. One thing I must say is to remember that love and walking in

Releasing Your Life

love is not a weakness! I used to think that to walk in Love meant being a doormat. That is the farthest thing from the truth!

Being in Love means you speak in love. You don't have to be crude when you talk to, correct, or disagree with someone. You don't stand and let people do what they want to do because you are afraid to hurt their feelings! There is a right way and a wrong way to do it. Most of it is common sense, because our nature in Christ is love. We shouldn't want any harm to come to others. We speak truthfully and tactfully, and then move on.

Move on to what? Move on to life, which is what we should be doing every day, shouldn't we? So what should we do? Wake up, build on our relationship with God, continue to converse with God, put God first, then go with God all day while walking in love.

Chapter Twenty-One

Questions and Direction

Where do we go from here, Lord? The top? The top of what? The top of the mountain? The top of the world? Heaven? Where do we go from here? The sky? Is the sky the limit? Do we have a limit? How many limits do we have? Our lives do not have to be so complicated. What are we missing, Lord? Are we missing everything? The entire point? Small points? Lord, give us some direction. Please, give us some wisdom. We know that you are coming soon. We know that we need to be prepared. You prepare us, God. You prepare us for where we want and, especially, need to be. We yearn to follow your will. We yearn to live in your ways. Thank you, Lord.

Thank you for your guidance. Thank you for all that you have to say.

Lord, we have so many rules and regulations in our lives today. It is almost like the Old Testament times, isn't it? But that is not your will. It cannot be your will. Your will is the New Testament. You are to write your laws on our hearts, as opposed to your laws that were written on the tablet for Moses to share. So what has happened, Lord? We are getting confused. We are getting confused, like the people were when you brought the Word, you brought it to life. *John 1:14 says, "And the Word was made flesh, and dwelt among us, (and we beheld his glory, the glory as of the only begotten of the Father,) full of grace and truth."* People didn't know what to do. They wanted to keep the old laws and yet believed that Jesus was the Messiah, the Messiah you promised to come and save us all.

Let us get it together, Lord. We don't have time for denominational divisions, rules, regulations that tell us who we are supposed to be in Christ. You are to tell us, God. You are to write you laws on our hearts. Lord, we need to simplify our lives. What are the basics? Why can't we live the basics? Draw us to you, Lord. Draw us close to you and never let us go. You have never let us go, have you? You have never left us or forsaken us, Lord, have you? Thank you for that. Thank you for all you did and have done. Thank you for your angels and what you have pledged or directed them to do. You are our source of inspiration.

Let us not make more rules or create more confusion in these end-times. Let us keep it simple, Lord. Let us constantly and consistently look to you. In consistency lies the power. Let us not grow weary or faint. Let us run with all that we have for the prize, the prize of the high calling of God. To be first in the race is what we seek all the time, Lord. *Philippians 3:14 says, "I press toward the mark for the prize of the high calling of God in Christ Jesus."* You are the keeper of our hearts, and once we have given it to you, we are forever comforted.

So we look to you, Lord. We look to you first. We look to you forevermore. We look to be your good and faithful servants. You are coming soon, Lord. Thank you for

Lana D. Tucker

fulfilling your Word to us, Lord. Thank you for remaining the same yesterday, today, and forever. You are right here every step of the way.

Chapter Twenty-Two

Praise

So let's take the time to praise God. Who is ready for your return, Lord? Who is ready to seek your face? We are! We are ready, Lord. We are ready to do as you would have us to do. We love you with all of our hearts and minds. You are justified by your Word, God, and by the trust we have in your Word. You are worthy to be praised. Dear God, we open our hearts to your Word. We allow it to change us and transform us to be like Jesus.

Thank you, Lord, for the day you have made today, this day. We will rejoice and be glad in it. You are the keeper of our souls, hearts, minds, and bodies because we have given them all to you. We honor you, Lord, with our existence as an example of what it is like to be like you. We strive to be like you, Lord. We strive to be all that you have created us to be, Lord. You are awesome, Lord! You are totally awesome! We love you for being you. We love you for making us! Thank you for placing us on this earth at this moment in time.

You have created us and our families for such a time as this, to be in this world now. Thank you for all that we are and could ever hope to be. To God be the glory for the things He has done for us. Thank you, Father, for all that you have done for us. We praise you, Father. We praise you with all of our being. You are worthy to be praised, Lord. You are worthy to be praised. Thank you, Father, for all that you are.

We thank you for simplifying our lives. We thank you for simplifying all of our lives as we prepare and work out our duties, to be fulfilled for your coming. Oh what a day that will be when you arrive in the clouds, when you come forth and receive unto you your children! What a glorious day that will be. For as the maidens were prepared for their bridegroom by filling their lamps with oil and having plenty more oil in store, we pray that we will be, too. We want to be ready when you come. We will be ready when you come to take us home. Thank you, Lord, for all that you have done and will do in our lives until you return.

Chapter Twenty-Three

Wrap It Up

You have given us everything that we need to be successful on this earth. That is successful in your eyes, in your way of doing things. Is it that we are confused and, as Christians, want to blend in with this world so that we have convinced ourselves that we must do things the worldly way first? Then I suppose we are meant to implement with magic a few things of God to be on top and to be something envied by the world? The truth is that Jesus didn't come into the world to blend in, did he? He came into the world to save sinners, regardless of race, age, economic background, health, wisdom, or any other differentiation we use. *Matthew 18:11*

(KJV) says, "For the Son of man is come to save that which was lost." He came and was in this world but not of this world, right? Right!

Jesus was not liked by everyone. I don't recall in the Bible stating that Jesus had a pity party. I don't remember him crying his eyes out because someone rejected him or hurt his feelings. He told his disciples to shake the dust from their feet and move on if they were not received by the town. We are supposed to do the same in this world. We are not to focus on the rejection, talk about the people, curse the people, hold a grudge, or not walk in love. We are to shake off the dust and simply move on. That's right, move on with life and the assignment that is laid out before us.

So do you know how much time we waste by internalizing our rejections? Way too much! So, dear Lord, I pray right now in Jesus' name that we do not internalize rejections. Besides, why do we expect better treatment than our Lord and Savior? He was rejected, so we should expect to be rejected as well. That is not our focus. Just because someone rejects the Word of God, the Gospel, the fact that Jesus Christ died for our sins and arose from the dead, does not mean that we have not planted a seed of thought in them, right? It is our part to share the message. It is not our part to be in the Holy Spirit's role to make them accept the Gospel or have their eyes opened to the Gospel, is it?

We have got to start making our lives simpler and incorporate less rules on ourselves. We have got to get on with the business of what we were meant to do. Our rules are like hindrances. It is like we fear what we are supposed to do, so we make excuses for why we aren't doing it. We probably aren't consciously doing this, but nonetheless, it happens. Please keep this in mind: Keep it easy! Keep it straightforward. Keep it uncomplicated. Keep it trouble-free. Keep it effortless.

Here are some things to keep in mind as a guide. It is my own guide. Remember, this is only a guide! Stop copying everyone and go to the Holy Spirit for your own guide, because he knows you more than you know yourself.

1) God first, period.
2) Never stop building your relationship with God through talking, praying, and reading the Word of God.
3) Walk in Love at all times.
4) You need people, too; cultivate and nourish relationships with family and friends.
5) Get moving! Live the life that God laid out for you!

These are the bottom line basics. These are not all of the basics. However, from these, so many things will fall in line with your lives. "Like what?" you say. You will build up your faith. Faith comes by hearing, and hearing by the Word of God. You will naturally fall in to the will of God for your life, which includes where he wants you to be and what he wants you to do. You will automatically be preparing for your future, unbeknownst to yourself because God knows your future and he will be preparing you along the way without your full knowledge. Remember, it doesn't matter that you don't know the details of your future. Trusting in

Releasing Your Life

God and following his lead will automatically prepare you. From the things above, you will also become more and more like Jesus without even trying to because of the works of God in you! When you are becoming more and more like God, your will is becoming his will because you will have further desire to be more like Jesus. This may not be an obvious, conscious decision of yours; it will just happen.

So work out your life. Put your life in an effortless mode by incorporating the basics. God first! Walk in Love! Period. Get down to the basics because Christ is coming soon. Keep it simple, keep it moving, and get on with releasing your life!

www.ingramcontent.com/pod-product-compliance
Lightning Source LLC
Chambersburg PA
CBHW031653040426
42453CB00006B/290